The Christmas Crayons

This book is dedicated to Maurena Crawford Williams for her endless LOVE and dedication to children.

A special thanks for allowing me to tell this story.

www.prgarcia1.com

It is Christmas Eve in Michigan.
Snowflakes trickle down from the sky.

A cold wind blows down the streets, and the snow is piled HIGH.

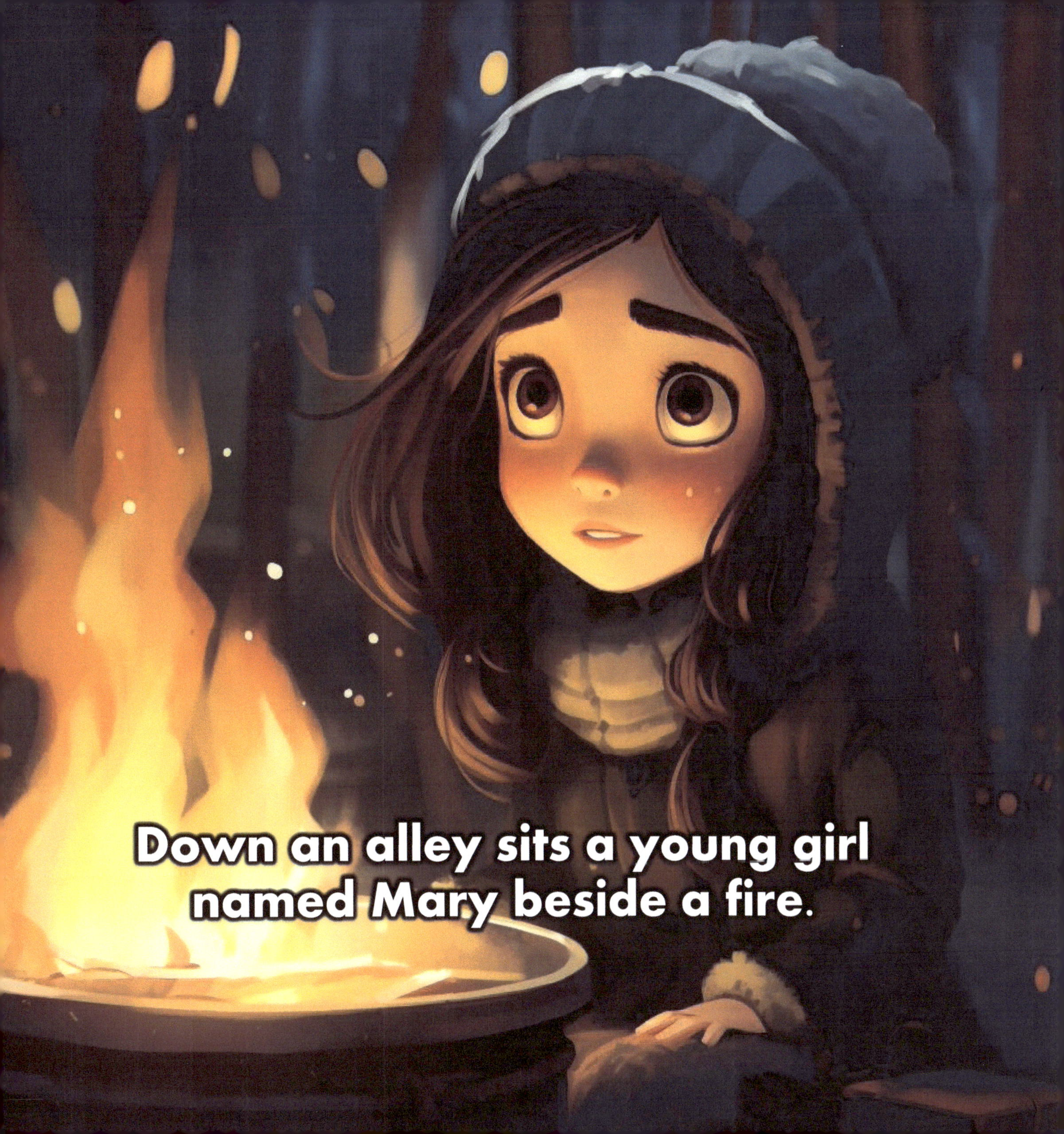
Down an alley sits a young girl named Mary beside a fire.

She is trying to get warm.

She and her mom are homeless.

Her mom is ill – she has a drug problem. She lost her job and could not pay the rent.

Mary shivers. She is very cold, but is afraid to tell her mom.

"Let's get out of this cold," her mom's boyfriend says. "I know a place where we can spend the night."

Jack leads them to an old empty house at the end of the street.

"We can stay here."

The house is falling apart. The paint is peeling off the walls. And most of the windows are broken.

But the walls block out the wind.

One of the men drags a barrel inside.

And another brings in firewood.

They build a fire in the drum. Soon the room is warm.

Tired and hungry, Mary curls up on an old mattress on the floor. She drifts off to sleep wondering if Santa will find her.

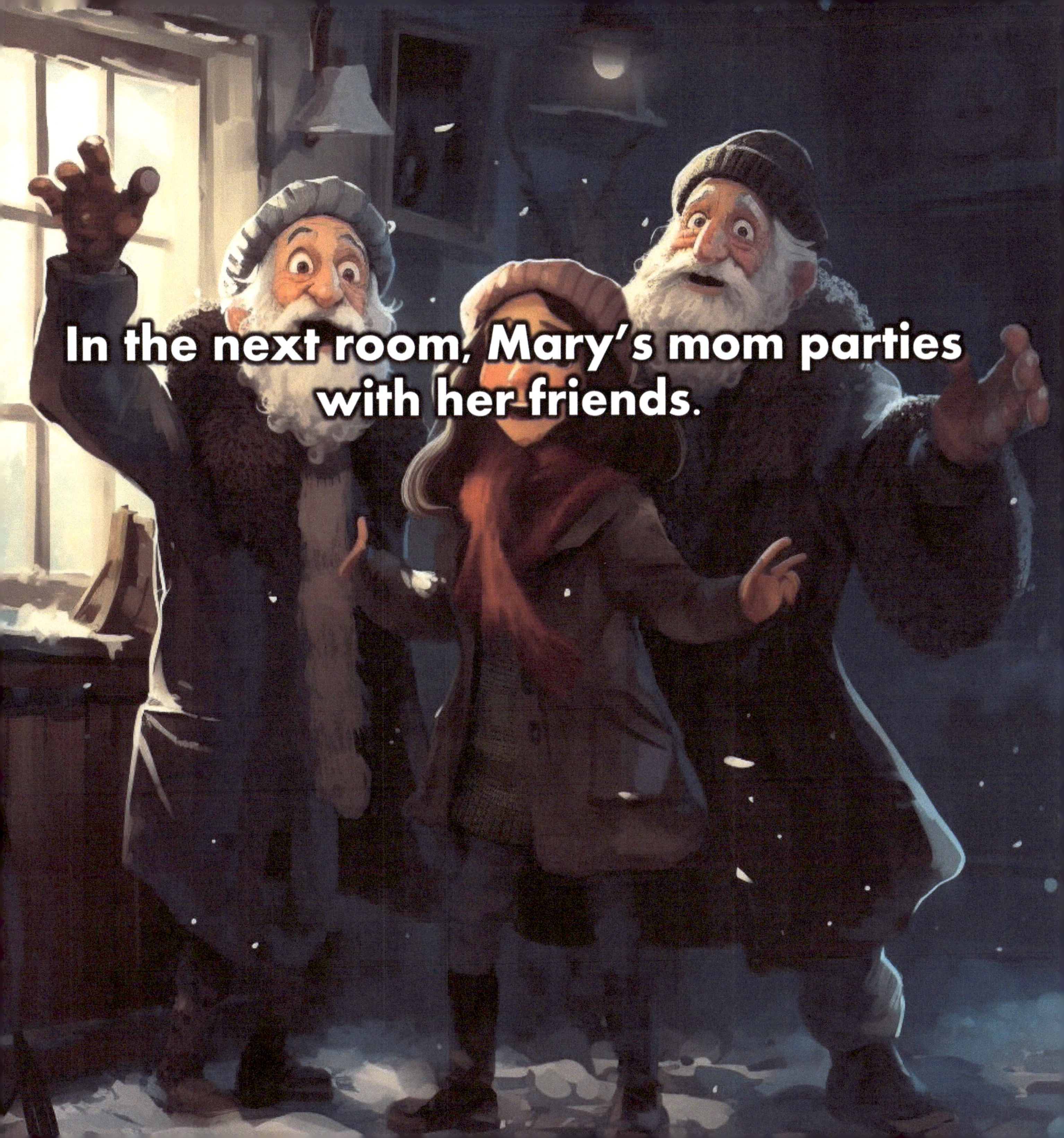

In the next room, Mary's mom parties with her friends.

Mary shivers awake. It's Christmas morning.

She opens her eyes. Did Santa come? Did he find her?

She runs into the next room.

There is no Christmas tree.

There are no presents.

All she sees is her mom sleeping on the floor.

Mary is sad.

Her mom AND Santa forgot her on Christmas Day.

"Hey, Kiddo," one of her mom's friends says.

"It looks like Santa came and left you something."

He reaches inside his pocket and gives Mary a box of crayons.

Mary is happy.
Santa DIDN'T forget her.

She looks around but there's no
paper to write on.

Knowing no one will care, she draws on the wall a big Christmas tree filled with lights and decorations.

Beside it she writes "Mary was here." She wants people to know she is real.

Later that day, Mary, her mom, and friends go to the local church for a Christmas dinner.

Mary is happy.
Her tummy is full and she's warm.

"Oh, yes! I'd like that," Mary says, a big smile on her face.

The kind man pays for them to spend the night at a nearby hotel.

That night, Mary sleeps in a warm bed with soft sheets and a fluffy blanket.

She is happy, but also sad. She forgot her crayons at the empty house.

There's no way for her to get them. Her one Christmas gift is gone.

Two days later a Social Worker comes to talk with Mary.

She tells Mary she is going to live at a new home. She will never be hungry or cold again.

And she will have a new Mom, a foster mom named Jennie.

Mary enjoys living with her new mom.

She now has lots of crayons to color with.

She is very happy.

The crayons remind her of the lost box of crayons Santa brought her one cold Christmas. And the happiness of making the Christmas tree on the wall.

Each Christmas, Mary and her new mom bake lots of cookies and breads.

They fill Christmas baskets with candies and their baked goods.

Mary always adds a box of crayons and coloring books.

Together, Jennie and Mary deliver the baskets to those in need at Christmas.

Mary is happy. The smiles on everyone's faces when they see the crayons remind her of her own Christmas crayons. And how a small act of kindness can bring so much joy.

www.ingramcontent.com/pod-product-compliance
Lightning Source LLC
Chambersburg PA
CBHW060843270326
41933CB00003B/183